Recondite

by Martin Allen

Recondite is a number of abstract digital pieces combined into one collection. Each series is based solely upon the source material sampled to create the overall pieces within the series. As a result sequential titles may be found in different series'.

Series 1

Alien

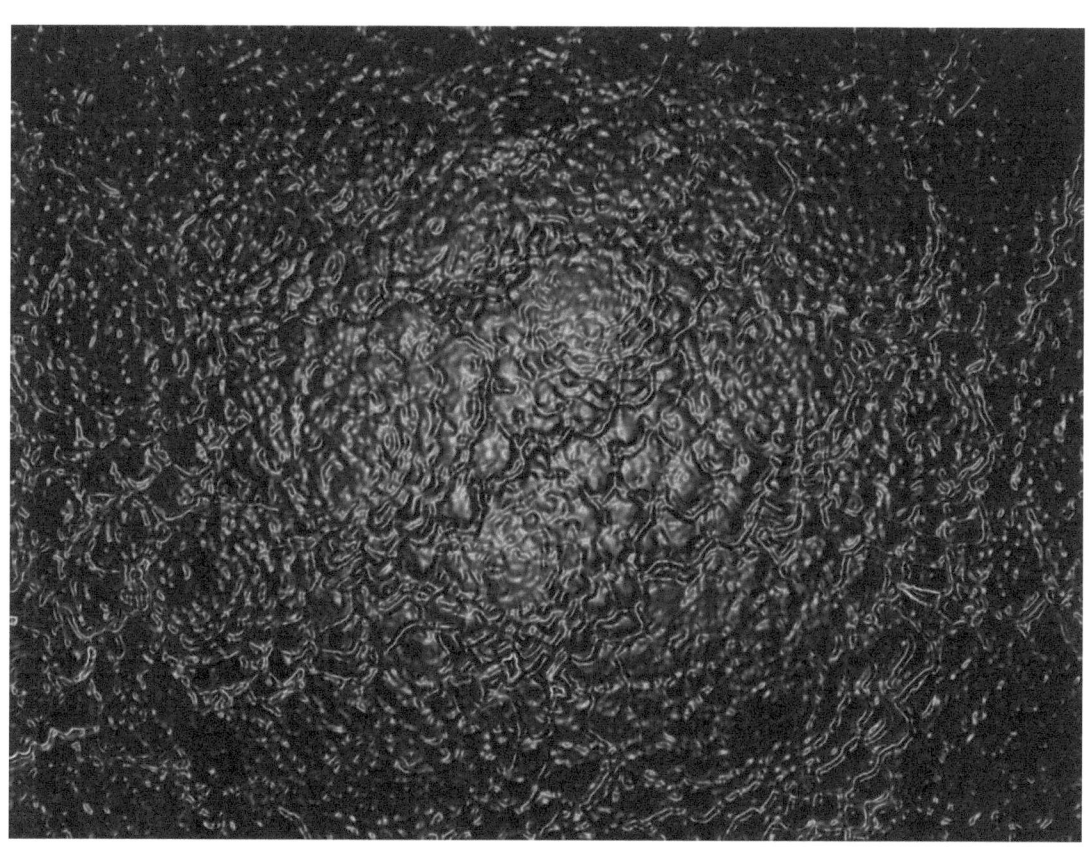

Alien Liquid

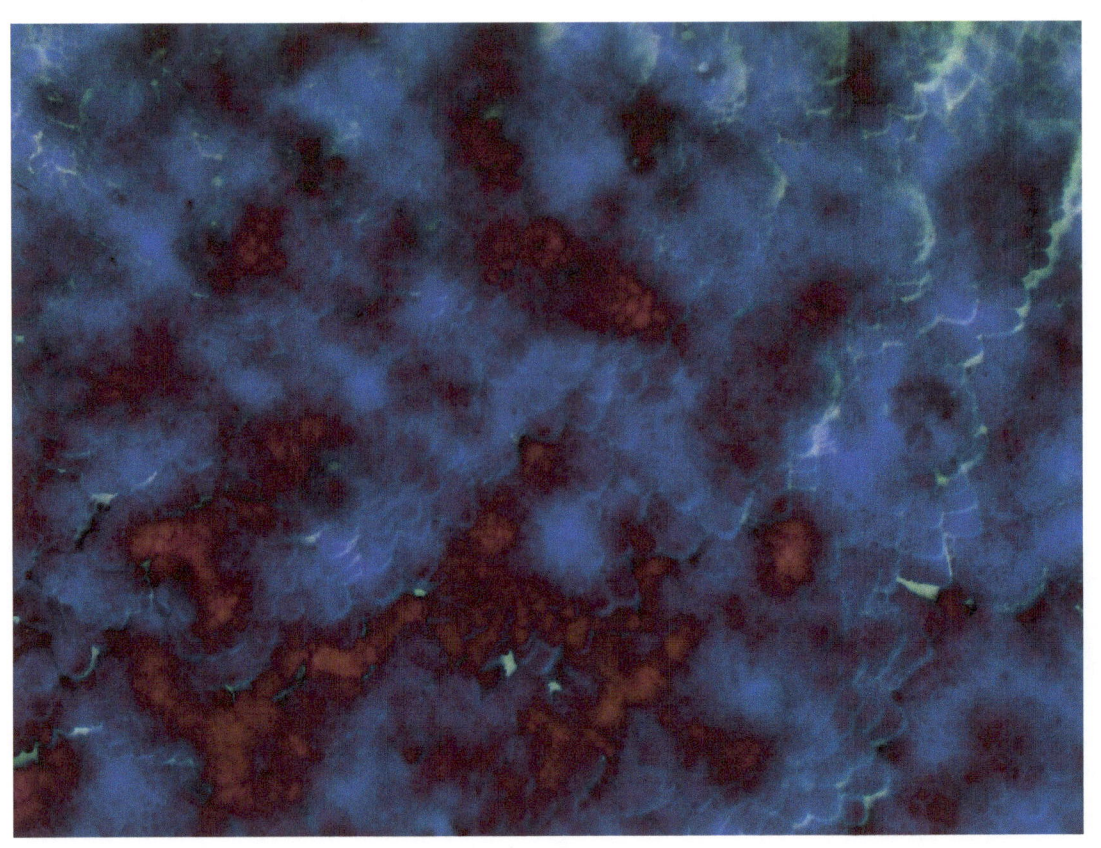

Fireset

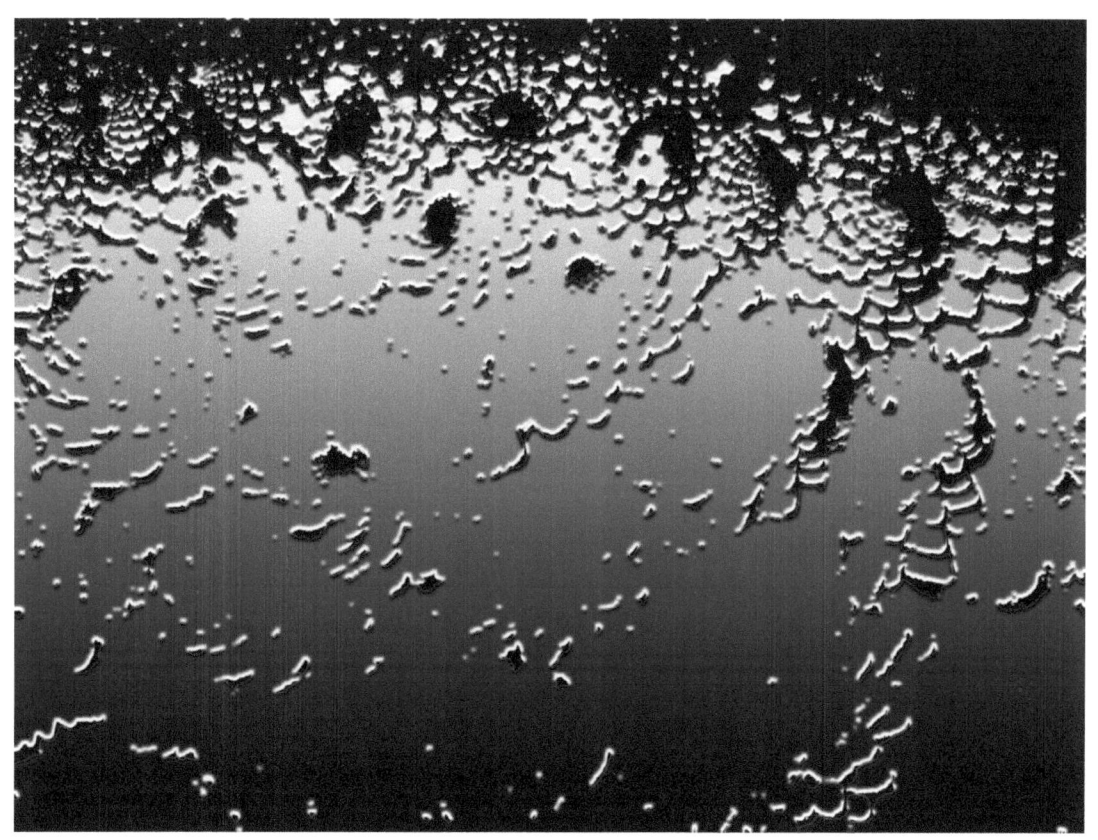

Greys

Series 2

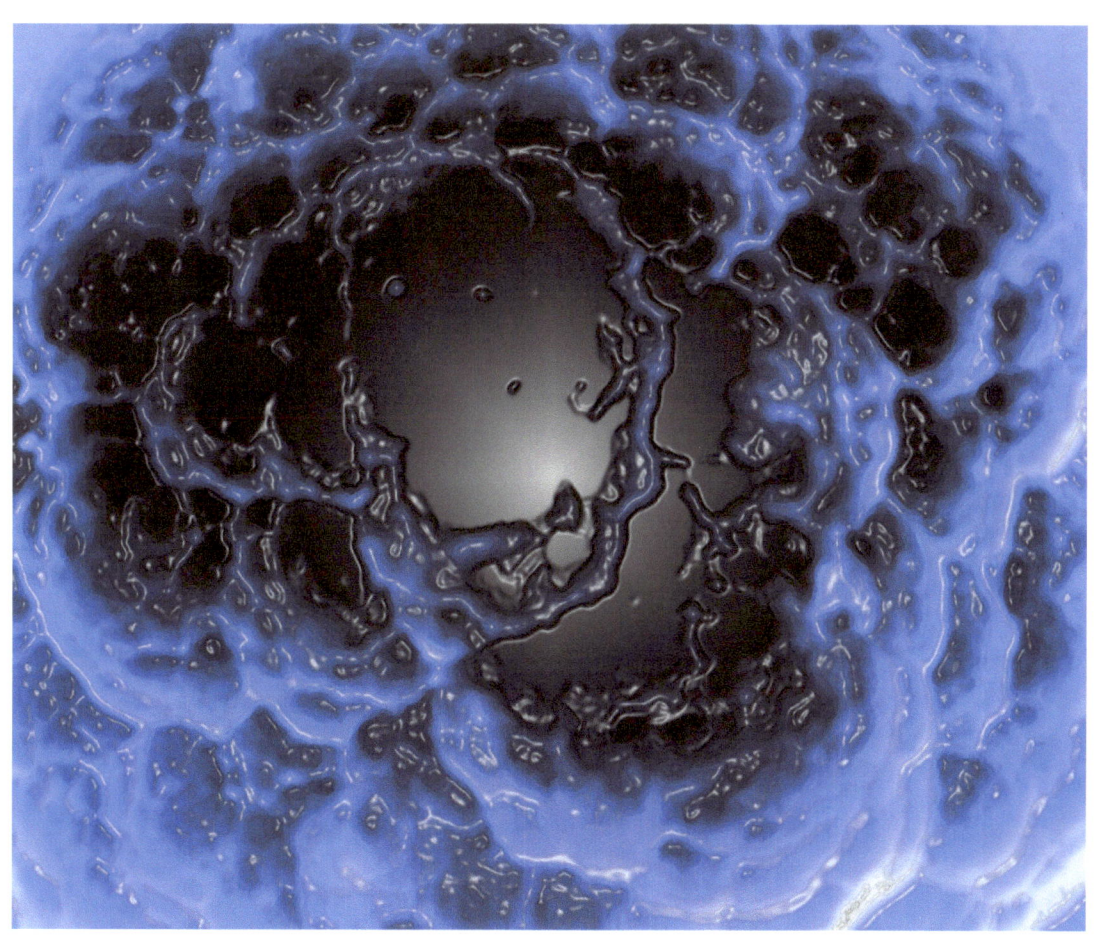

Blues

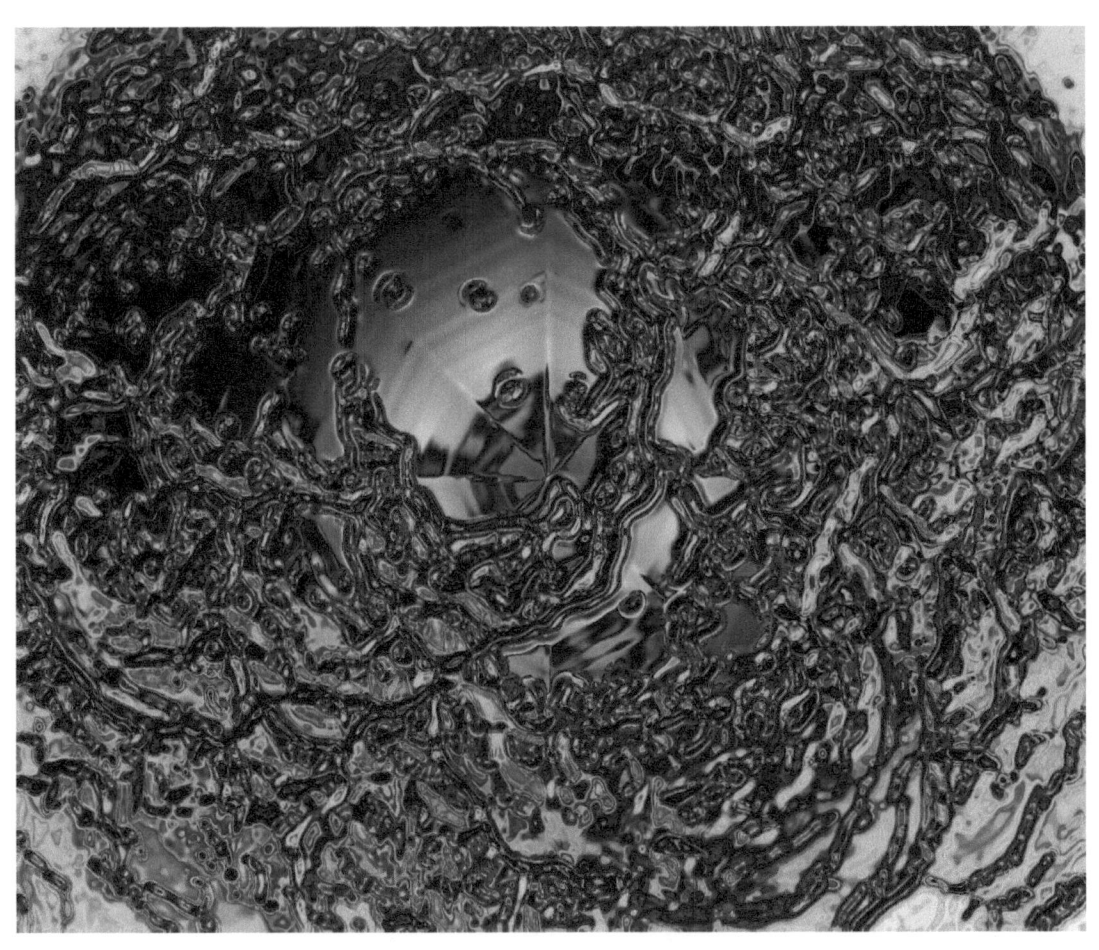

Diamond in the Rough

Series 3

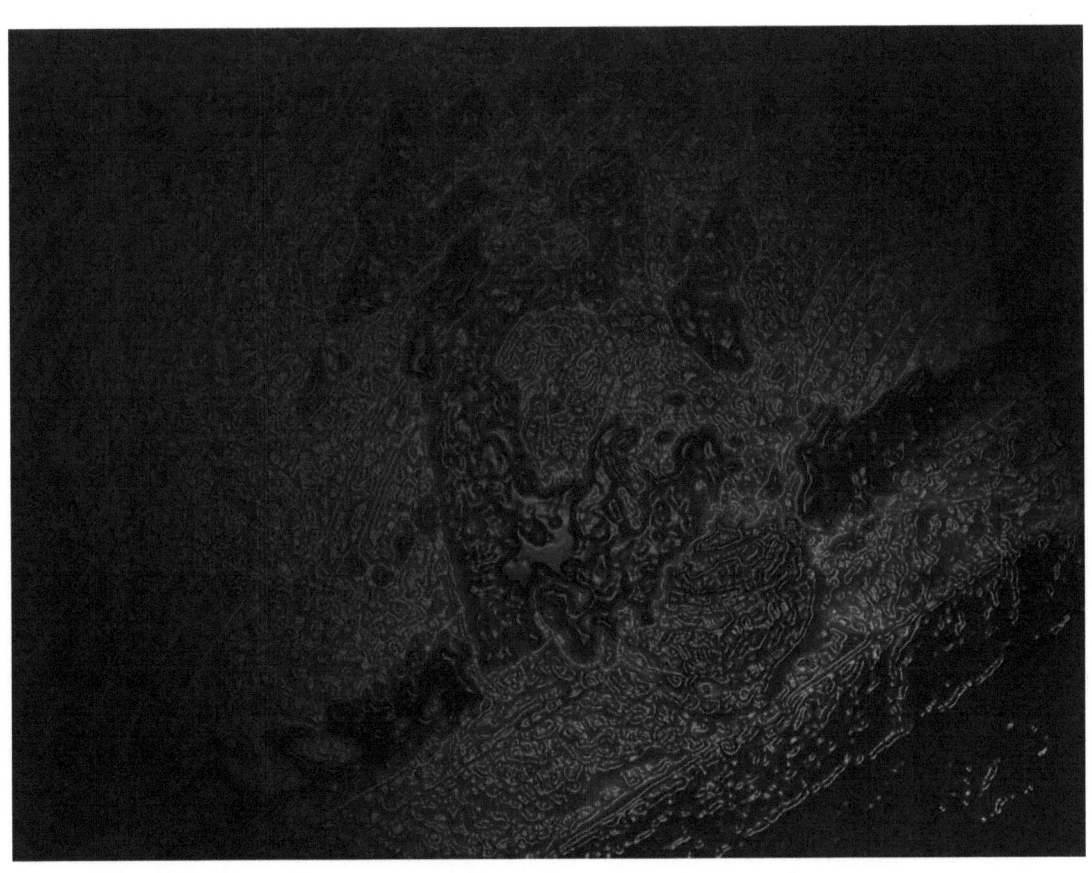

Blood on the Dancefloor

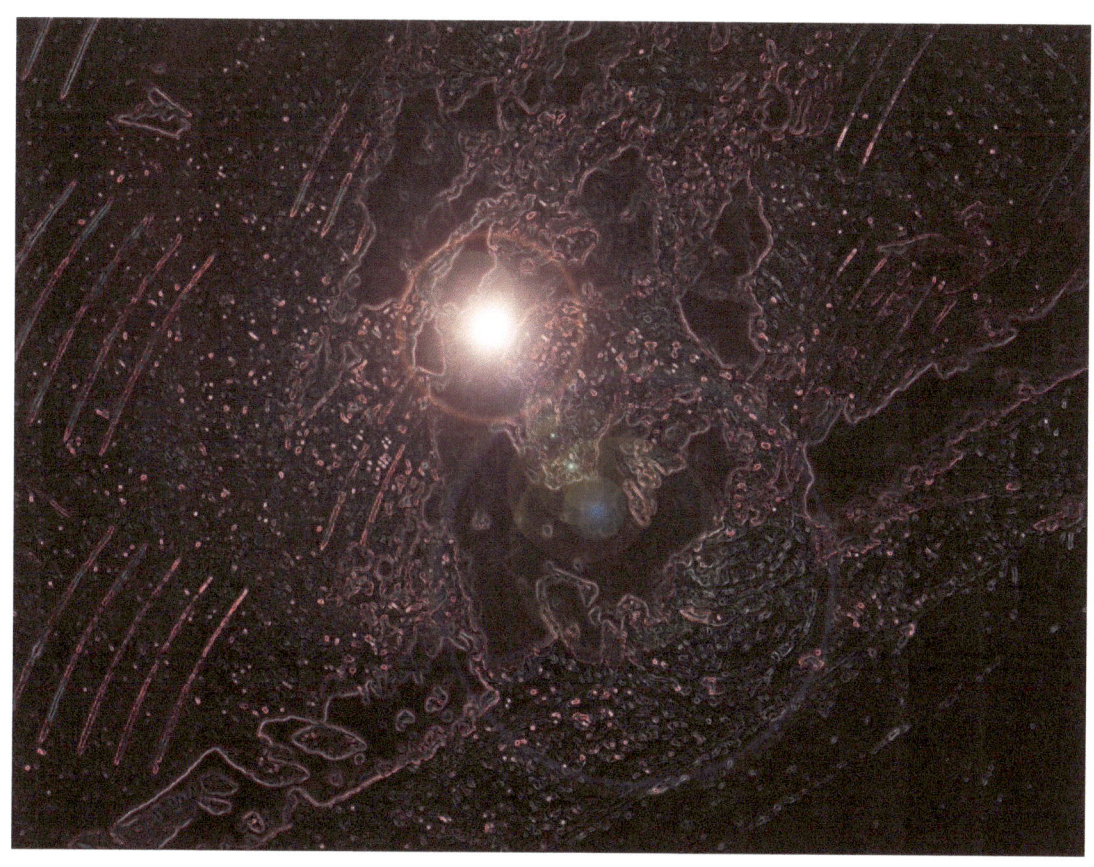

Corrosion

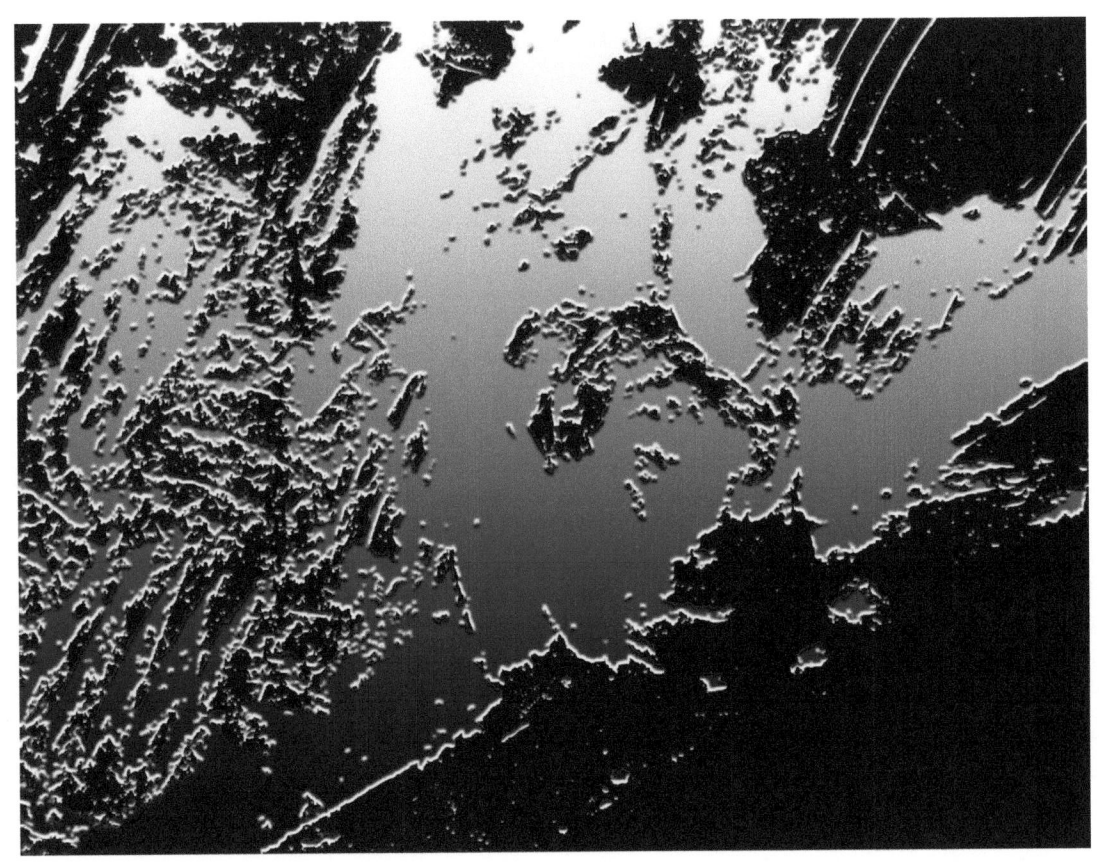

Vortex Storm

Series 4

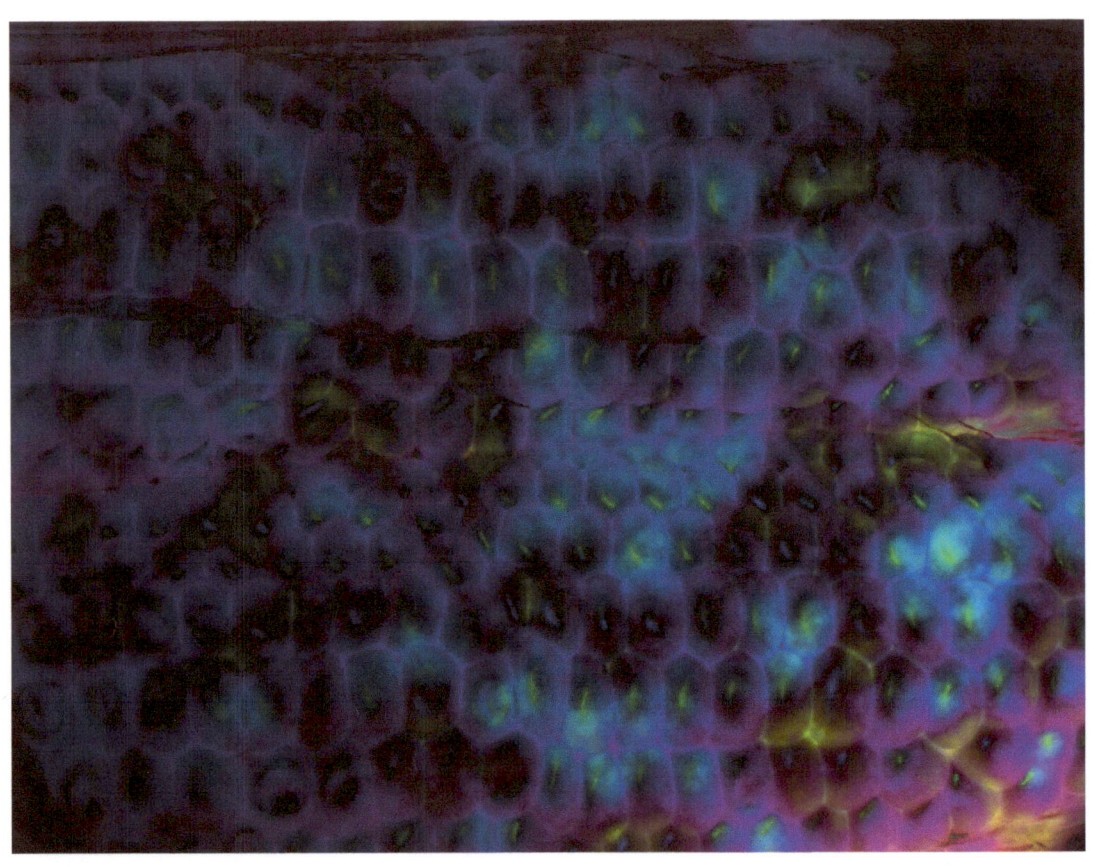

Storm Cell

Series 5

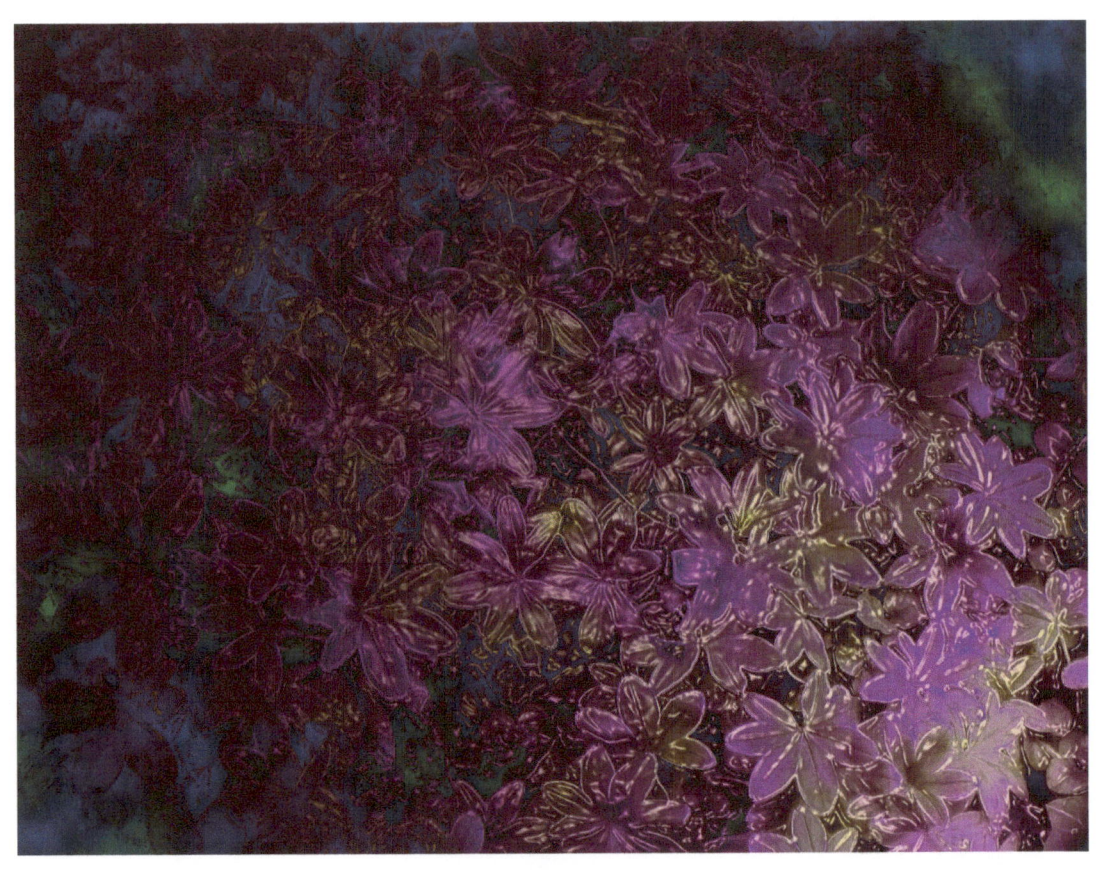

Royal Leaves

Series 6

Ghost Fern

Series 7

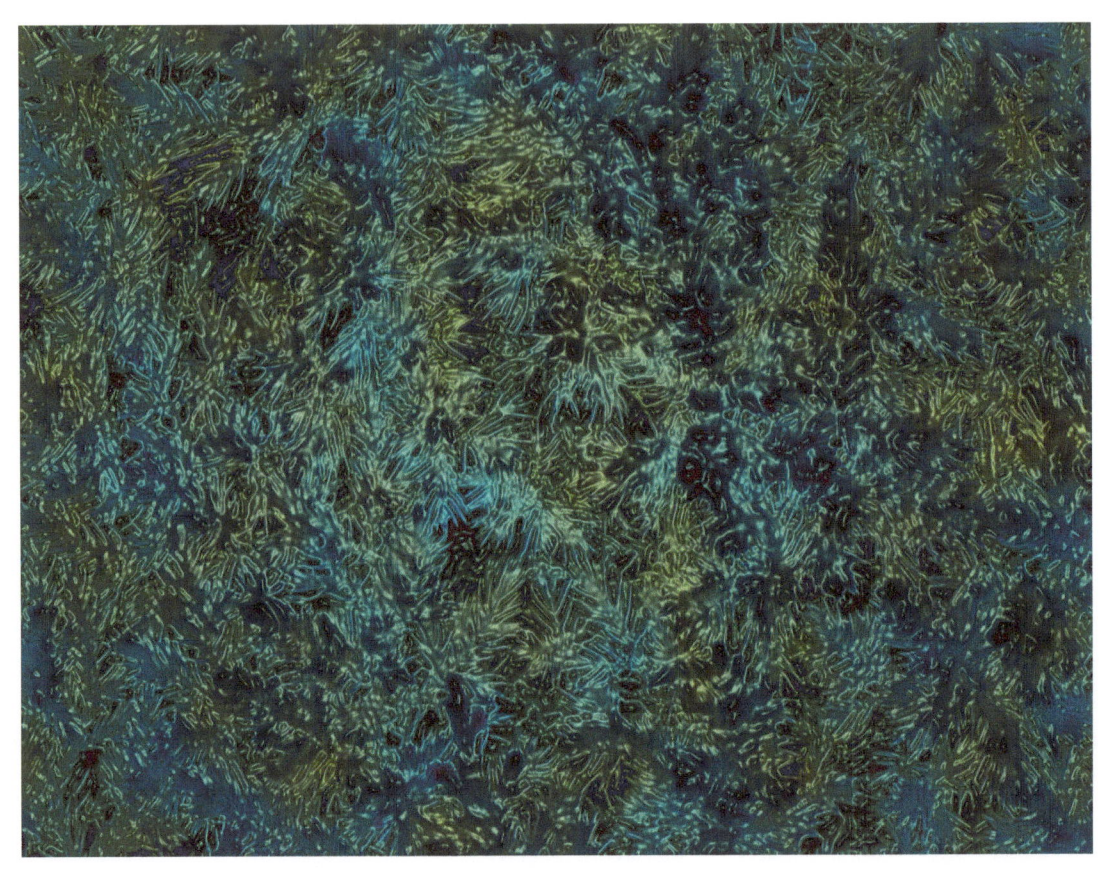

Royal Green

Series 8

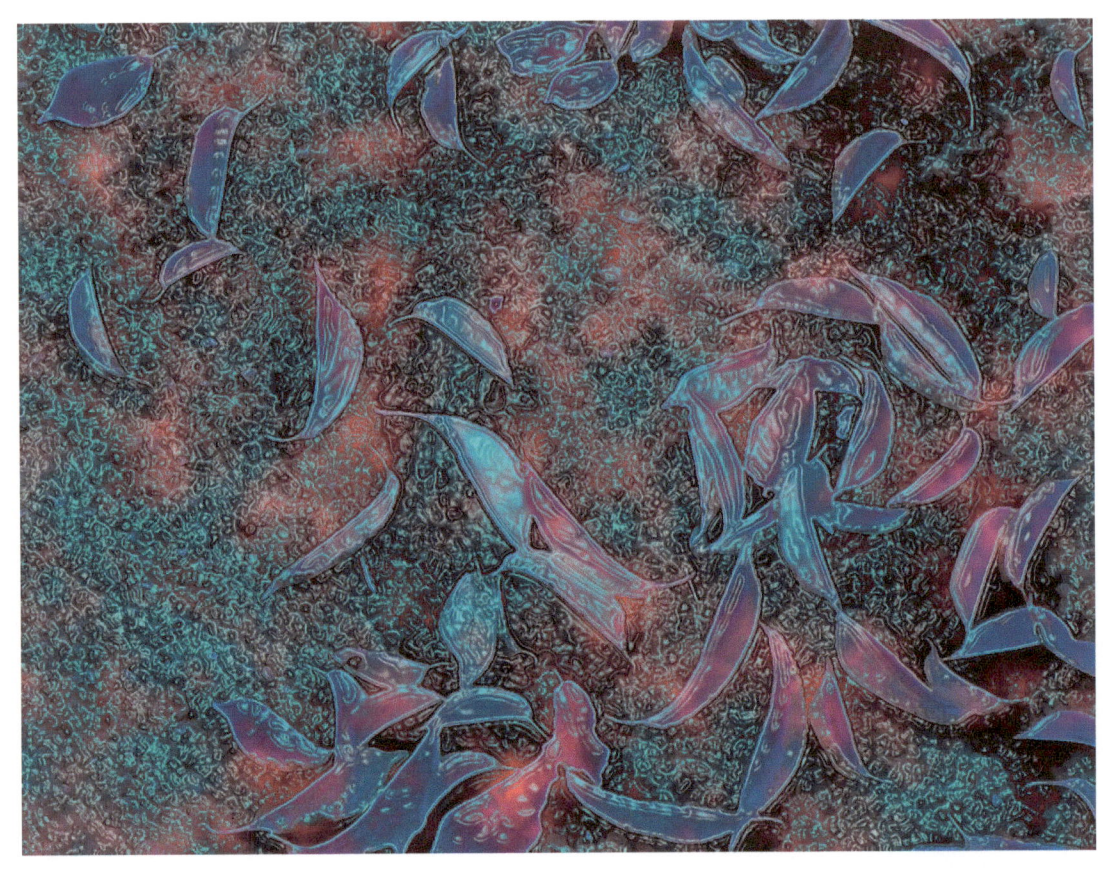

Plastic

Series 9

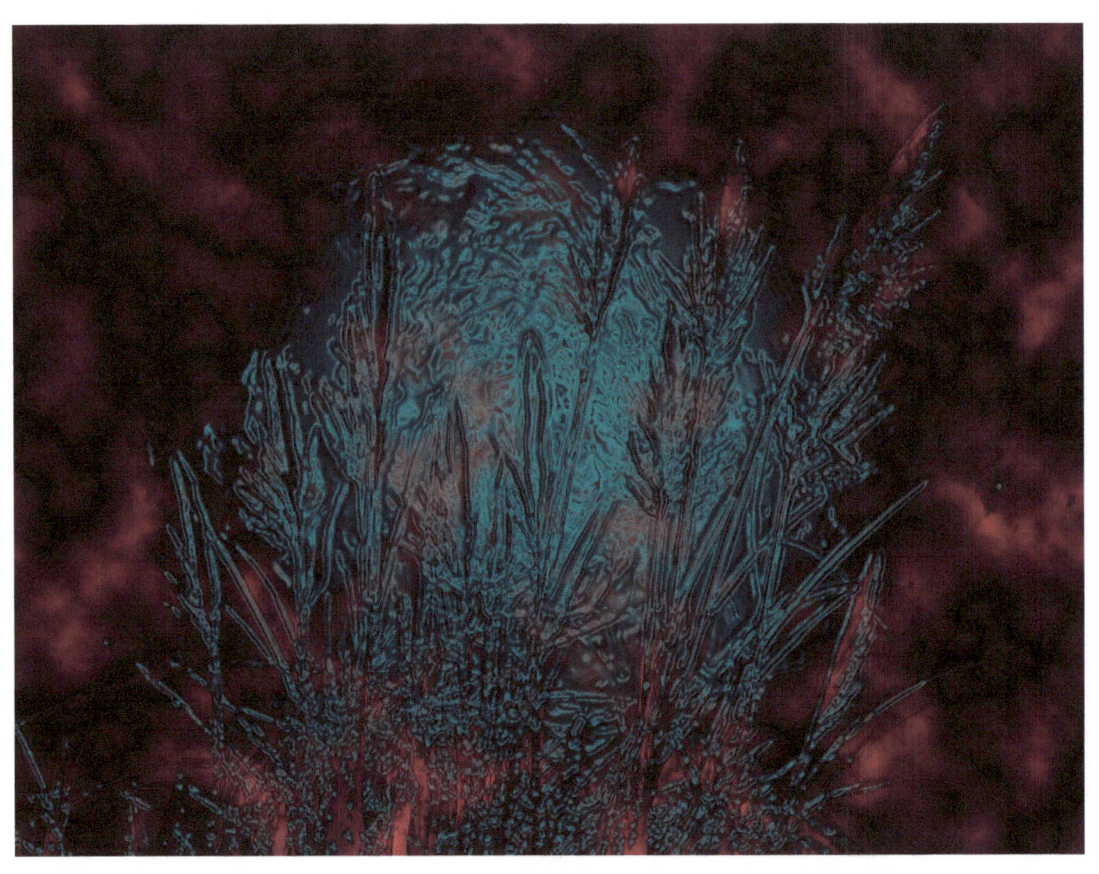

Dark Moon

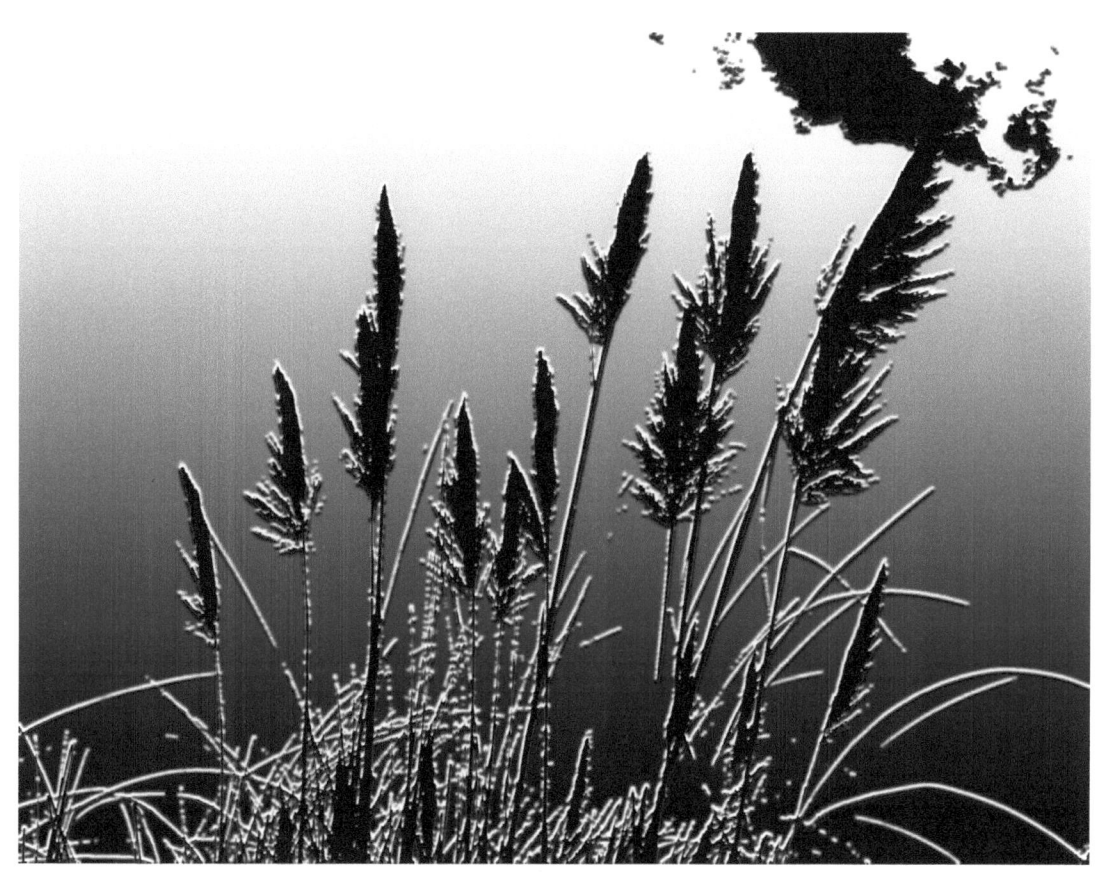

Grey Spears

Series 10

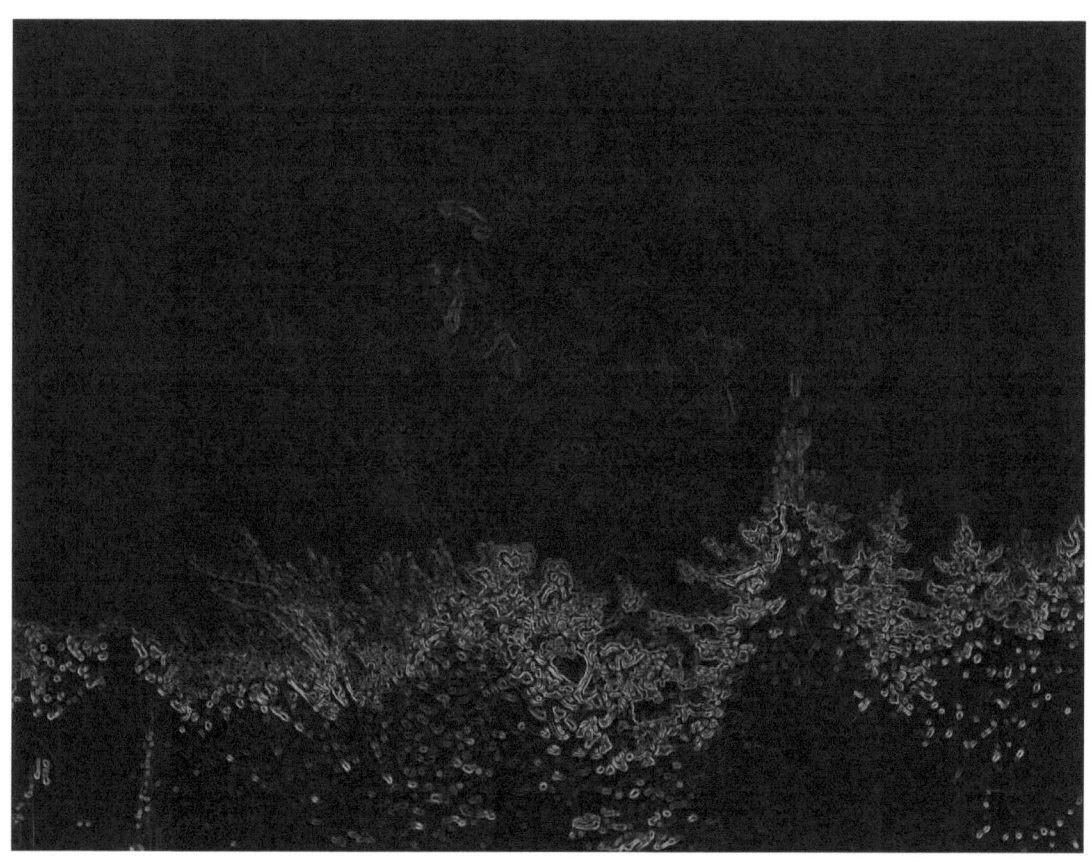

Beast

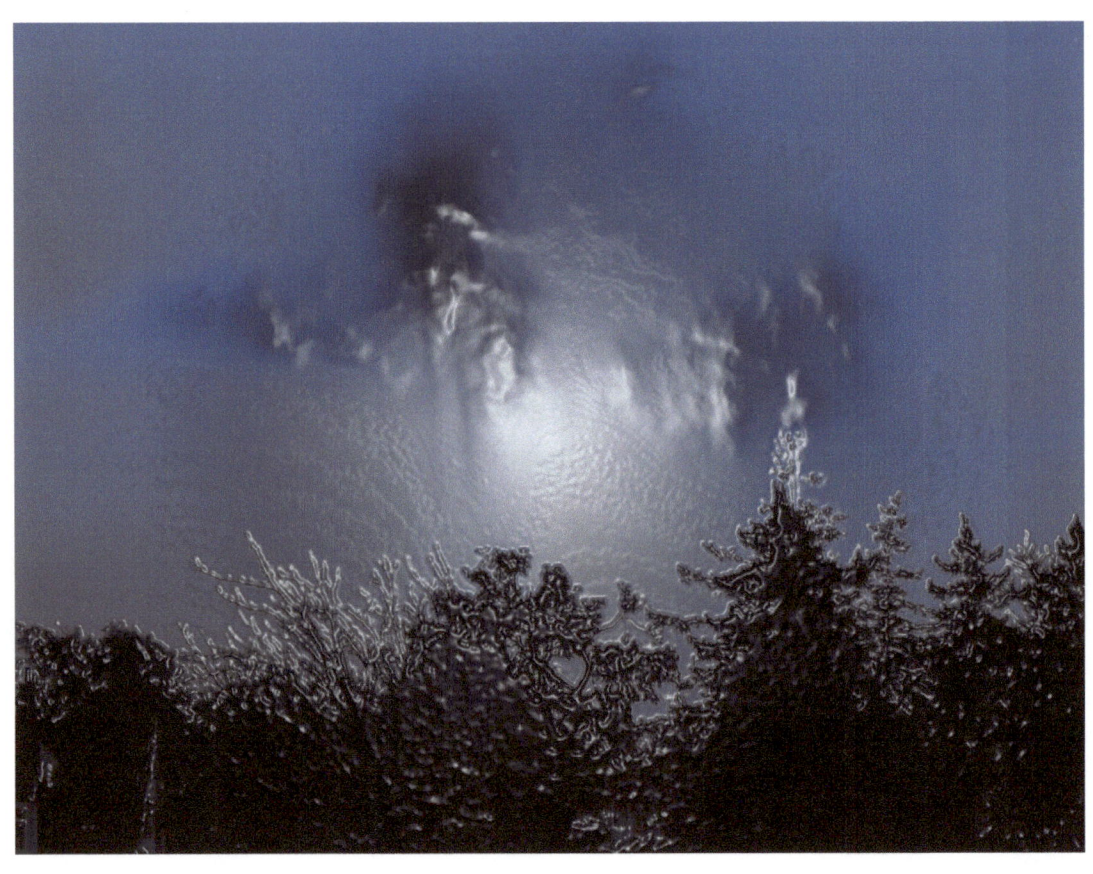

Blue Push

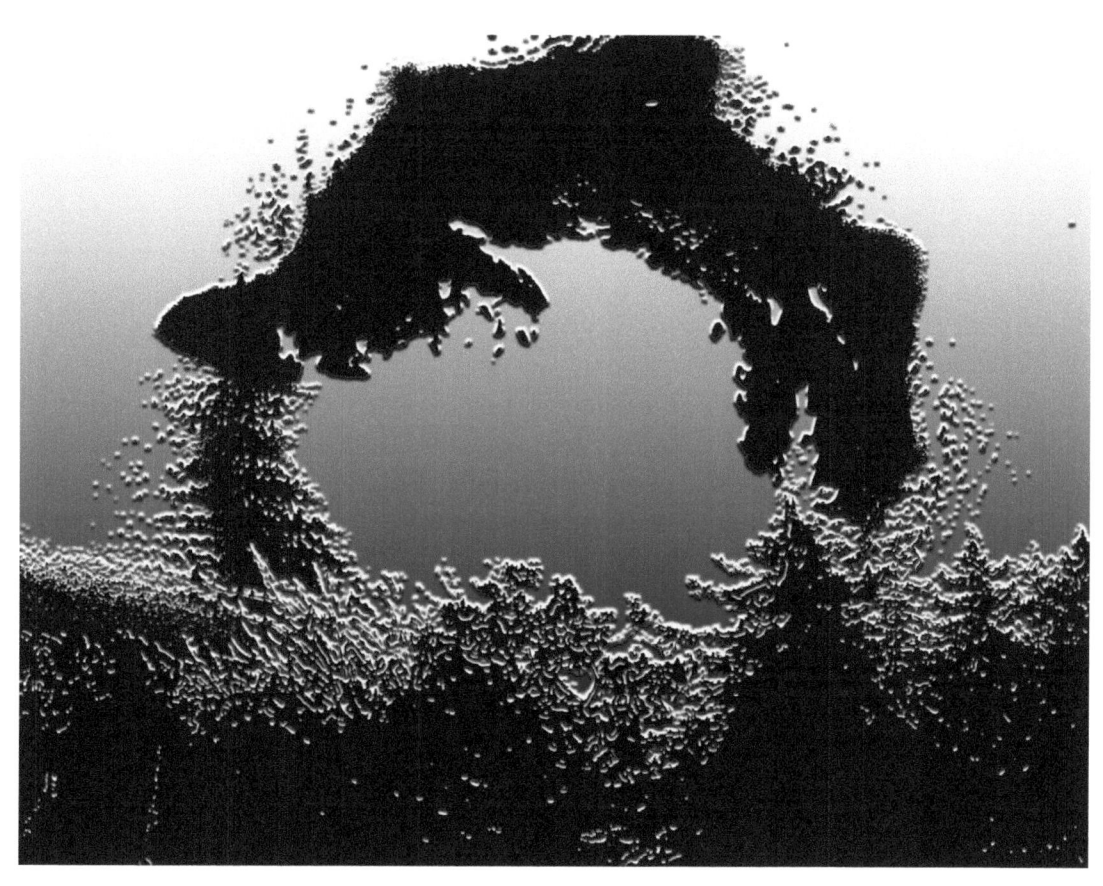

Grey Halo

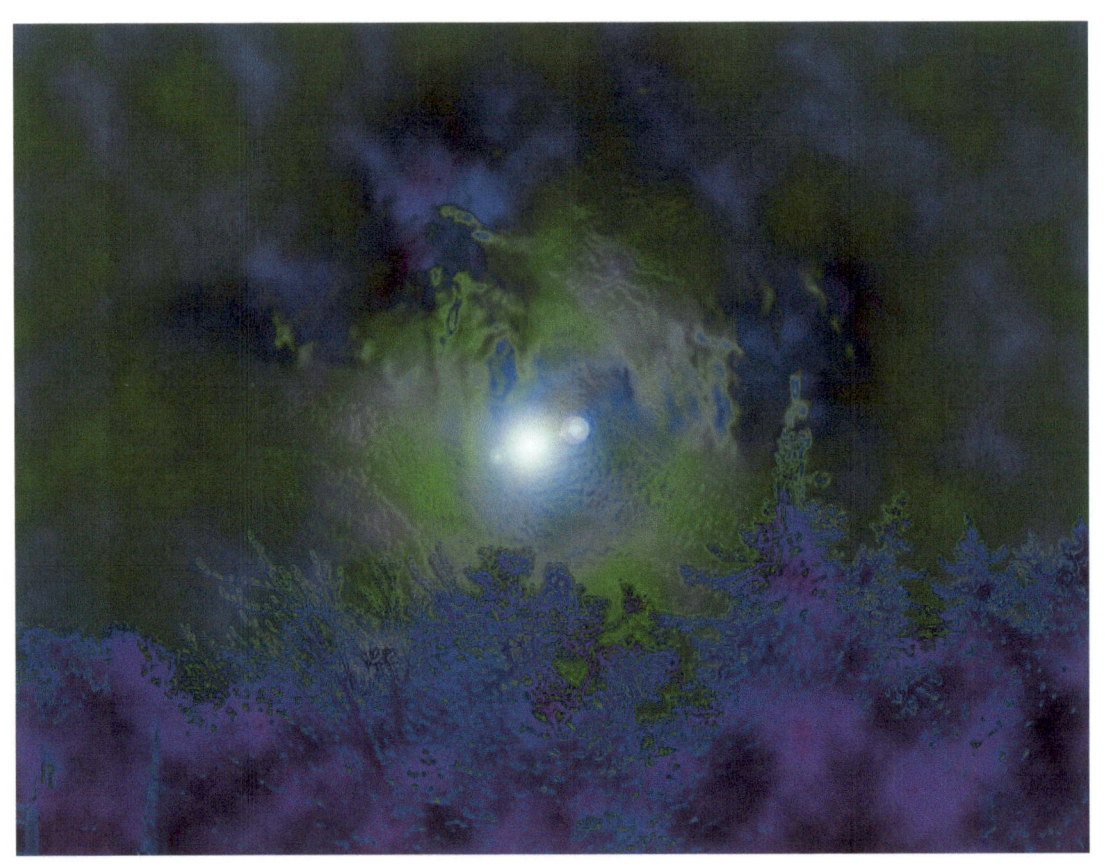

Wyrmhole

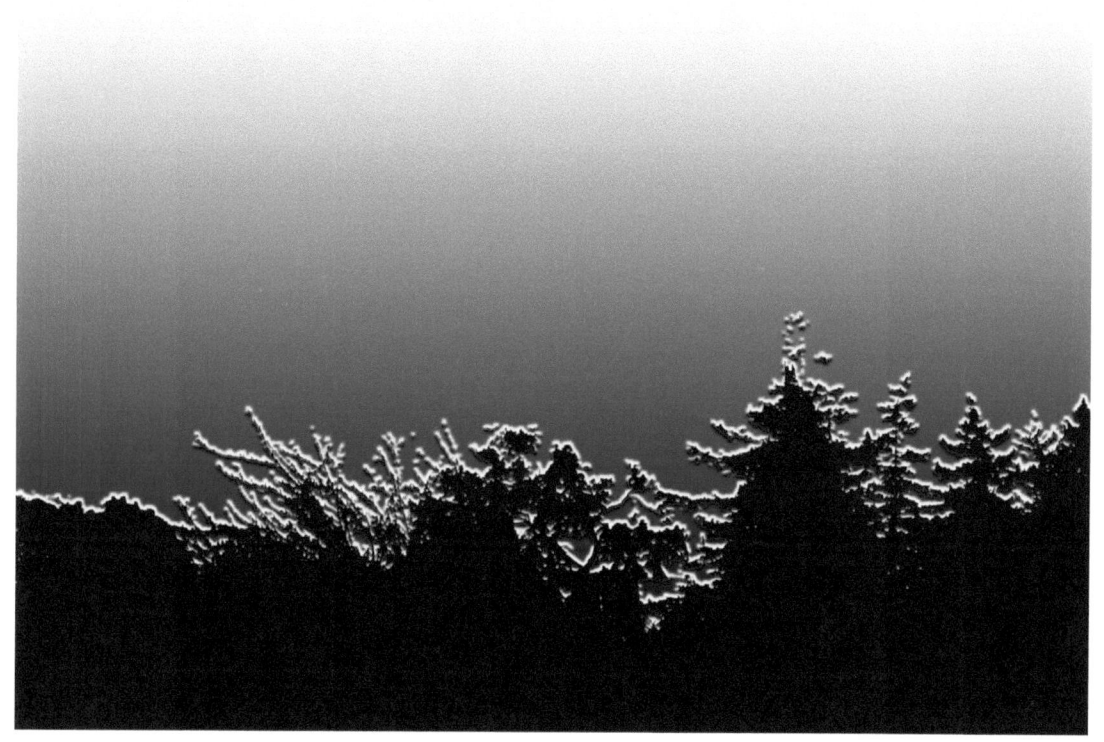

Skyline

Series 11

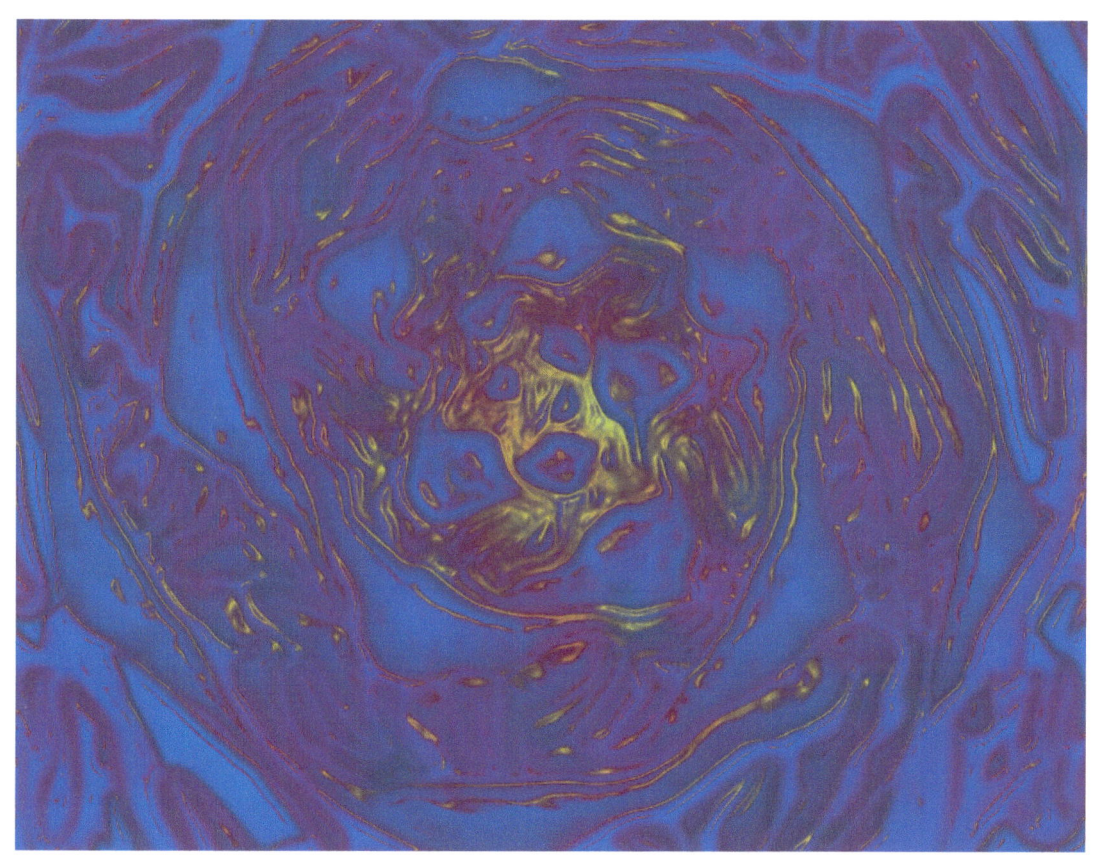

Blues 2

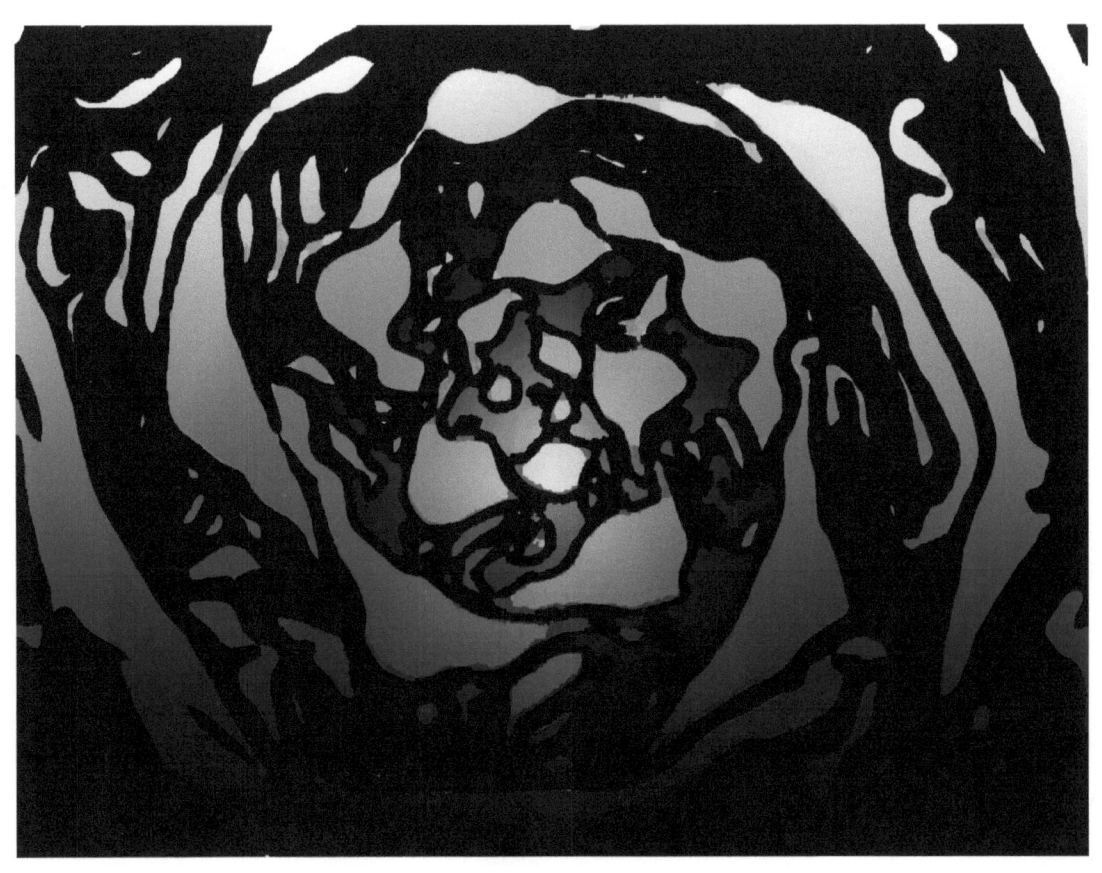

Tribal Cartoon

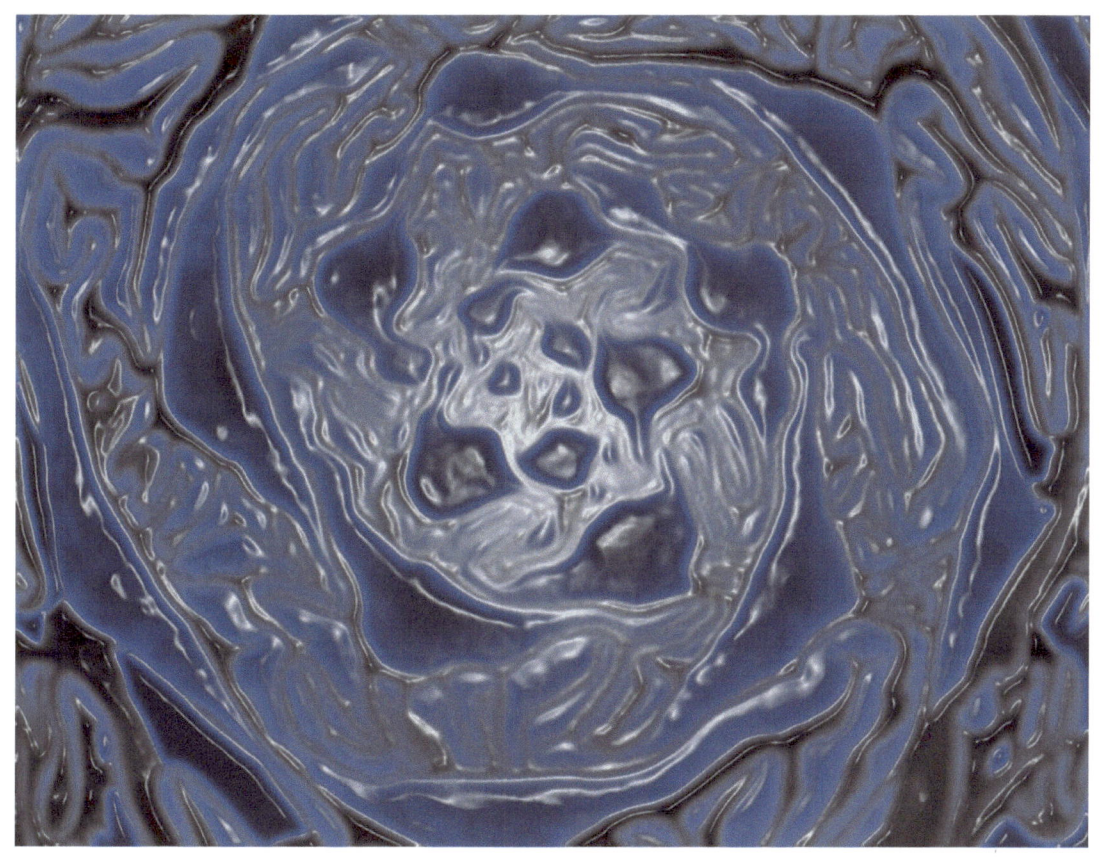

Cold

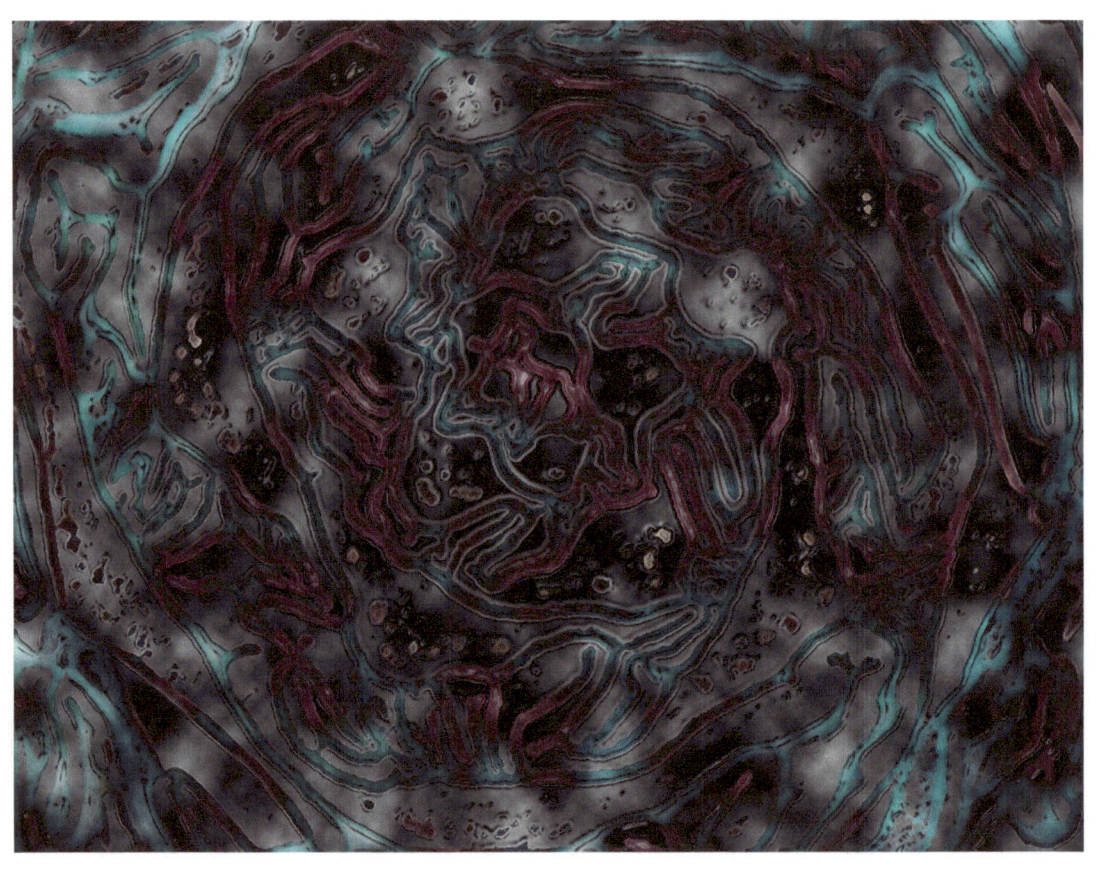

Dark

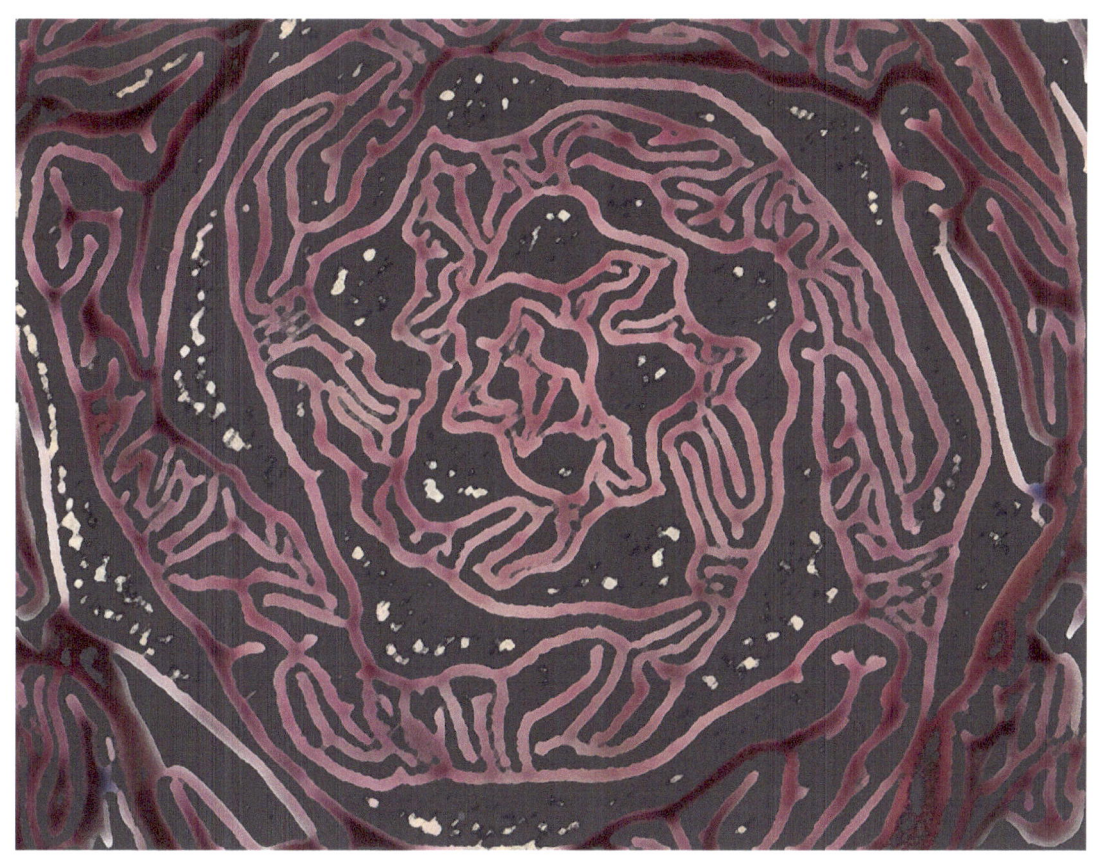

Pink

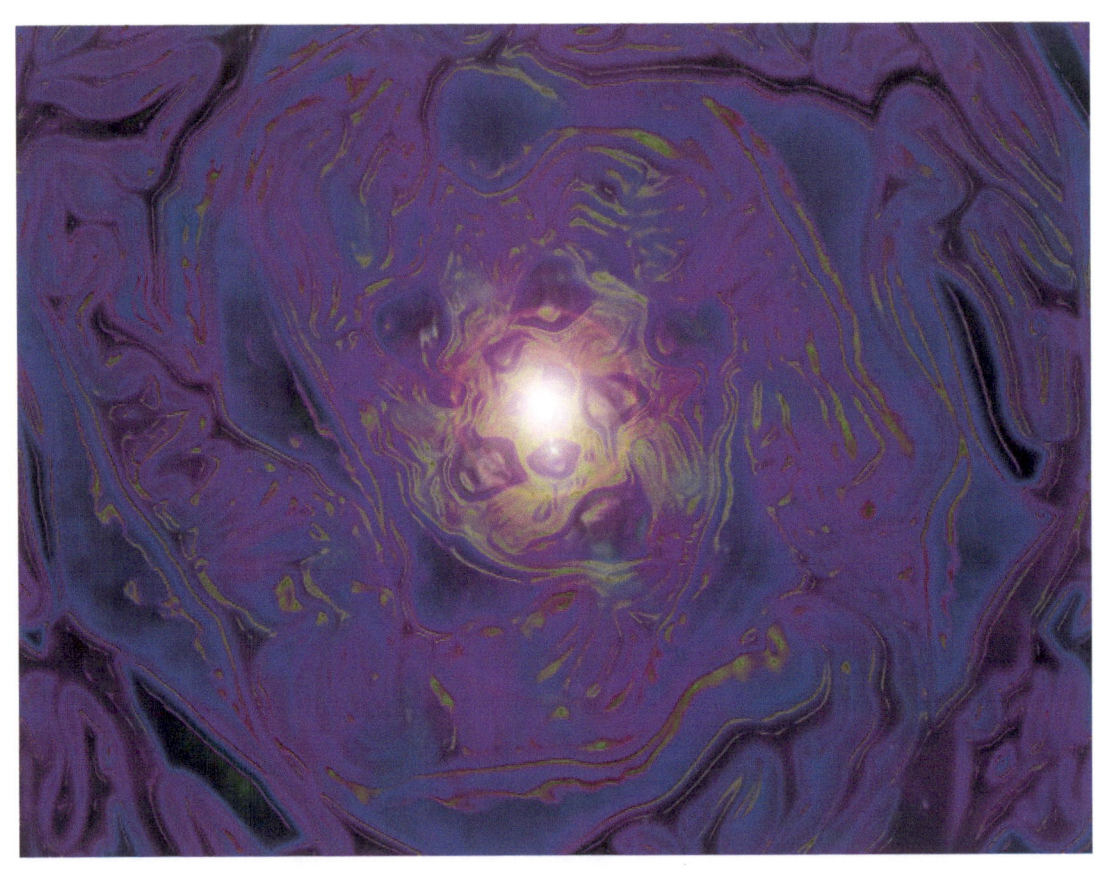

Wyrmhole 2

About the Author

Martin Allen graduated from the University of Northumbria at Newcastle in 2003 with a Law LL.B (Hons) Exempting L.P.C. Degree. He has worked in many different areas of the Legal Sector and built up a wealth of experience.

Martin enjoys reading and writing Science Fiction but has taken the time to wrote a few Legal pieces, one of which is available in E-Book format through Amazon (The Prosecutor's Fallacy: The Reliability of DNA and Fingerprint Evidence).

The Phoenix Series is a Science Fiction series set in a world where a Theocracy has come to power. "Phoenix: Penitence" is a short story set in this world. The first Novel "Phoenix: Rising" charts the rise of a new interpretation of the theological teachings of this Empire and the lengths this Empire will go to protect itself from it. The story is told from the point of view of an Imperial Investigator caught in the middle of the Empire's manoeuvrings.

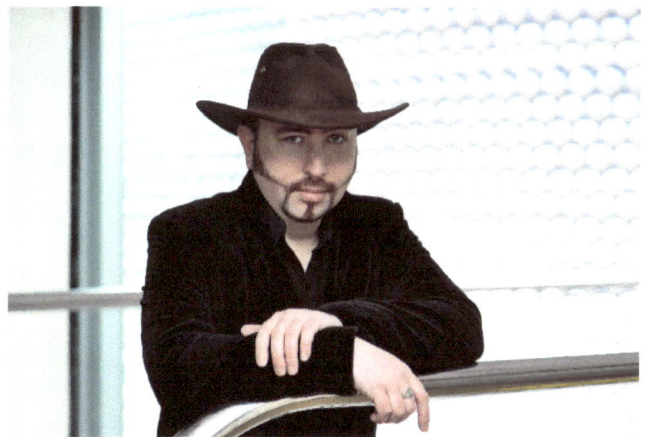

Photograph courtesy of www.jagjohal.co.uk

Other titles by the Same Author

Factual:

The Prosecutors Fallacy: The Reliability of DNA and Fingerprint Evidence
****
"The author has delivered a thought provoking, well researched and eminently readable overview of the perils of regarding DNA/ fingerprint evidence as 100% definitive proof of innocence or guilt. Rather it makes the reader aware that scientific evidence is conducted by humans and is therefore is fallible. Ideally forensic evidence evaluation is a tool to relate a likelihood ratio of a combination of diverse factors towards the guilt of a suspect. It enlightens the reader to the hazards of over reliance on science in an adversarial courtroom setting without stifling the reader with jargon or requiring advanced knowledge of Bayesian statistics and it would benefit legal & forensic students to purchase a copy as an introductory text (plus its cheap). Since publication the Forensic Science Service has closed and forensic analysis is contracted out to labs, therefore evaluation of the conviction rate in relation to the prosecutors fallacy and the evidential value of DNA or fingerprints bears close scrutiny to prevent any miscarriages of justice." – Scott Walker (Amazon.co.uk)

Science Fiction:

Phoenix: Penitence

Phoenix: Rising

**** - "Very Interesting Future Depicted"

"This book takes place in the distant future. Earth has had a tragic event and is now dominated by a single Empire. In fact, this Empire has been spread to outer colonies (other planets), and draws it's strength and authority from the teachings of one specific religion. As with previous empires on Earth, searching for those that would bring it down is left to a trusted few - and it is one of those trusted few that tells this story." – J. Heyman (Amazon.com)

**** - "A Fun Read no matter who you are"

"I cannot tell you how much I loved this book. It is a science fiction book, but it doesn't feel like one. Usually, in my experience, when it comes to a science fiction story, you are either following a space crew as they explore the deep reaches of the unknown but this novel took the original approach on focusing on religion. If there were not any references to colony planets or plasma weapons, I wouldn't have guessed this fact at all but I think that is something that really works for this story.

The plot of this story is heavily influenced by the New Testament. You can probably guess what story specifically by the plot synopsis. If not, then you will recognize the story the second you read the first reference. Despite all that, the ending is not as predictable as you think it would be. It felt like the first time I have ever heard the story, which is great.

Also, should make a comment on something. This book is not very dialogue heavy, but you get a big picture on what goes on in the protagonist's head. That, to me, is a more important aspect in books because this is the only form of media where you can get to know your main character inside and out completely.

I highly recommend this book to all those who want a different approach to the science fiction genre, those who are interested in learning a bit more about religion without digging into the bible, or those who want a refreshing take on an old story." – Scott (Amazon.com and Book Junkies)

***** - "Brilliant"
"This is well written, structured will and well worth reading. Faultless. Both myself and a friend have read this and we both agree this is a good read." – Laura Hartless (Amazon.co.uk)